CONSTRAINTS

✽

CONSTRAINTS

STEFFAN TRIPLETT

NEW MICHIGAN PRESS
TUCSON, ARIZONA

NEW MICHIGAN PRESS
DEPT OF ENGLISH, P. O. BOX 210067
UNIVERSITY OF ARIZONA
TUCSON, AZ 85721-0067

<http://newmichiganpress.com>

Orders and queries to <nmp@thediagram.com>.

ISBN 978-1-934832-92-9. FIRST PRINTING.

Design by Ander Monson.

Cover image: 213047371 © SHEIN DMITRII
DREAMSTIME.COM

CONTENTS

I am keeping myself company.
—Aisha Sabatini Sloan

APARTMENTALIZING

In a show I know never filmed a proper ending, a cheerleader gets the teeth knocked out of her and the rest of the squad can't stop dreaming up images of blood. "Do whatever it takes to rid yourselves of what happened to her," the coach tells them. *Do whatever it takes to rid yourself of what happened.*

✦

An admission: I am finding it difficult to let go of still feeling like a teenager. A tougher admission: last year on New Year's, my partner asked if I wanted [   ] and I was so in my head that I cried. My therapist says I still carry guilt for something I shouldn't feel guilty for.

I am still getting used to having long hair. One day, I dream my curls long enough to pull back into a loose puff.

One day, I awake and they are.

I am letting my hair grow to see all that it can do. Or, I am letting my hair grow to keep track of the time. Or, I am letting my hair grow because I am fearful of change.

As a writer, I've learned to like the routine of excision and display. I can't tell if my strands are falling out more quickly than before or if I just have more to lose. In the shower, when I wash them, I remove brown webs wrapped around my knuckles and place them on the opposing wall.

✦

Time is always a confused tense. I am afraid I *am* receding with my hairline / I am afraid I *will* recede with my hairline. These seem the same but I sense a distinction.

If it's gone, will I still look like me to you? I don't look how I think I should look in the mirror. A recent thought I am embarrassed is recurring: once it's gone, will I still look [   ] to you?

It took me five years of dating to want to live with a partner. The night I moved in I expected to feel, wholly, that I'd made the wrong decision. The feeling never came; I am still getting used to feeling happy.

I see a hair on the shower wall and for a second, I am not sure if it's my partner's or my own. My coffee mug reads, "The Future Is NOW" and I don't know whether to be encouraged or scared. I am avoiding thinking about the future.

I promise these things are all related because they all make me feel the same, I go to write in a journal. Or, a student articulates it better than I can: *this feels like it's navigating a hallway of opened and unopened doors.* Or, "He was attacking," a girl says in a show I used to love but no longer have the taste for, "or maybe he was just talking."

One day, the hairs on the wall start taking on forms of their own. One day I see a face—eyes, a mouth, hair made of hair. In it, I imagine a host of expressions.

Each time my father needed a haircut, he would drive an hour-and-a-half one way—he liked the barbershop our own town couldn't offer and, also, I think he liked the drive. I understand the sentiment. Being stuck inside feels the same as being states away from home: I just feel like I am lacking context.

I devour a show about a ship stuck in ice. In it, a young man is persuaded that in death there's nothing to be afraid of. Or is it after this life, it's *nothing* to be afraid of? I feel affirmed to watch the men grow accustomed to horrific constraints.

*

Do I still sound like me to you? One day I think I hear a shuffling. I say "hello?" to no one at all.

I've been inside for months and somehow a [   ] still murders someone new. It's all over the news; it's always trial all in the air. I miss being in communion with my friends.

I don't ever want to be in a house with a gun. I don't ever want to be outside a house with a gun. I don't ever want to be beside myself with a [   ].

I like being alone, I think just days before feeling extreme loneliness. On another New Year's, I call my partner to say I can't bear the thought of another year of anything. When they ask what I mean, I don't have an answer for them, just the feeling.

I love my partner and they are nothing but loving to me. Some days I am so comfortable I could seep into the walls. What I mean is I am terrified of fading one step closer toward a pale, empty nothing.

My partner has a bad dream, so bad that they cry after. I am left to wonder what it was—it's miserable to imagine all the worst things that could happen to them. Later they tell me, it was quite straightforward: their family and I were all in a car that drove over a bridge and into a [ ].

I nightmare all the time, but this affects me more than my own. What a sad idea it is to disappear in the mind of someone else. For a moment I understand that here, I am a loved, lived being; context— even if it looks different from the old.

✦

In a movie I return to, a woman
who looks like family doesn't
die but turns into leaves. Veins
sprouting, blood turning root.
One moment she's there walking
through trees and then, suddenly,
she's

ON A BRIDGE

Here was a church I had gone to, there another, and there one again. Pointing them out to Marc was an easy way to fill the awkward silence between us. Each time we passed one that I knew, I kept one hand on the steering wheel, excitedly pointing my index finger through glass. I had struggled to find enough interesting things to do to fill an afternoon in my hometown: Scrabble, Starbucks, a tour of the mall, the little art museum, the churches. That seemed to cover everything the town had to offer. I had planned the park as our last destination.

The two of us followed the sidewalk that weaved around a play structure, like the one I bloodied in the fourth grade. Young and clumsy, I had tripped and slammed my face into a plastic, hexagonal roost. I bit deep into my lip, teeth breaking and busting out. I was silent at first, then felt a stinging, saw the blood, and began to wail. *Is he gonna die from this?* a classmate asked my teacher. I told Marc this story as we walked, praying he wouldn't find me boring. I told him stories of all the times I'd been to this park before, how my grandmother used to babysit and take me and my cousins here, how friends and I still came here at night during the summer, swinging back and forth until we needed to make curfew, and about the time a nearby resident called the cops on me, suspicious of the young man in the car.

An invisible rope pulled my stomach towards Marc, though I made sure not to stand too close. I was seventeen and I remember thinking this is what a real crush must feel like. I kept my hands in my black zip-up. In the nighttime the light from the streetlamps didn't reach this far. We followed the path to one of the only areas that was lit: the little bridge near the gazebo. He stopped in the middle of it, leaning against one side of the bridge. I mirrored his actions, leaning on the side opposite from him. I stood there, unsure of what to do next.

The grass was still alive and green in December. Marc stood up from the wooden rail. He was directly across from me, beginning to close the gap between us. Someone from the neighboring houses across the street could see us if they looked hard enough. God could see us. Two hours earlier, Marc told me he couldn't live in a town so small, so conservative. You have to come to Kansas City, he said. His hair was black and swirly, and hung out from under his beanie. The dark waves rolled around his forehead as he moved. This is where his heritage showed the most—the hair of his Mexican father. His skin was pale this time of year, lighter than mine, which too had faded in these months without much sun. The trickle of the small, man-made stream looped in the background as the beginning-of-Winter chill surrounded us. He inched closer. His eyes were looking right at me. I held his glance, then looked away, not knowing what to say. I kept my hands in the pockets of my hoodie and shifted against the rail. He kept smiling and I tried to see anything but lips. His jeans were dark and skinny, the same pair he wore when we met on a college visit a handful of months before. His figure was petite, and I saw its edges defined in the layers that hung on his torso.

"I want to kiss you," he said.

My stomach squeezed into itself. I stood up straight and inched off the rail. I thought about what to say, but no words came out. It wasn't a question. It required no answer. The space between us tightened as he moved closer. All feeling went to my temples, and I watched the place where his words left pulling in like a magnet towards me. His smell surrounded me, and I felt breath and body heat.

Then I felt a boy's lips on mine for the first time.

For a moment, I didn't move. I took in the shock and the feeling of this pink warmth. I tried to match the movements of his mouth. My teeth knocked his. I laughed for a moment then pulled away. He laughed too, then saw I was no longer smiling. "What's wrong?" Looking down, I shoved my hands in my pocket, and headed back to my car in silence. He followed. I fumbled the keys and got in the driver's side. Marc got into the car and shut the door. He probed, asking what was the matter.

"I don't want to be doing anything that's *wrong*."

His mind worked for a response. Despite my hesitations, his presence made my heart flitter. "This isn't a sin," he pleaded, breath floating between us. Wanting to believe him, I asked again about his youth minister, the one he said knew Marc was attracted to men, and said that God wouldn't care. He assured me that she did exist, that she indeed had said those things. He started kissing me again. Enclosed in the car I could smell his cologne. A little like vanilla, and a lot like the woods. He smelled like comfort and warmth. Smiling, his eyes were closed. I closed my eyes hoping to feel the same. None of this felt real. I tried to let my thoughts drain as I focused on the feeling. But I was worried about the police and the park's curfew. I told him about the time the cops came, again. Urged him to come back to my house. "It's your car," he said playfully, gently.

Heat filtered through the air vents as I started the car. We left the cold at the park, toasting up. While we drove back to my house, he reached for my hand across the center console. I turned up the CD I burned the night before, trying to impress him.

"I want to know your plans
and how involved in them I am.
When I go to sleep for good,
will I be forgiven?"

✦

Back home my parents were already asleep. Marc was spending the night and driving back home early the next morning. We decided that we would watch a movie downstairs in the living room. He wanted me to choose. I fingered through my dad's collection in the laundry room cabinets. I chose *I, Robot*. Feeling a need to explain my choice, I told Marc how my dad and I were really into Sci-fi.

"I'm really into Will Smith," he responded. We laughed.

Where would I sit on the couch? He was sitting on one end while I put in the DVD. I thought about what I watched friends do with their significant others over the years. I sat down in the middle. I wrung my hands in my lap and he, sensing my inhibition, immediately put his legs across mine. I put my hands on his shins. We sat like that for nearly an hour. "Are we actually going to watch it all?" Marc asked. He took my shrug as an invitation and moved his head towards mine. I looked away from the translucent robot on the screen and leaned in to kiss him back. I felt a little better now. I ran my hands through his hair. It felt like cold silk. Almost like mine did when I was just out of the shower, but a little smoother. "Your Chapstick tastes good," he said. I figured he was trying to help me relax.

"I'm afraid my parents will hear," I told him.

He kept kissing me, and I tried to ignore thoughts of what my parents would think. He lifted his shirt over his head and put my hands on his chest. I let myself touch the hairs that sprinkled. He assured me that it would be fine, we'd hear them if they were coming down. This would stay my secret. The credits started to roll.

"Are you ready to go to bed?" I asked.

The TV silenced the room when I clicked it off, and we quietly walked upstairs. We brushed our teeth, and I liked the image of the two of us together in the mirror. I peeked through the crack in the door to make sure my parents were still asleep.

In my room, I made a pallet on the floor and gave Marc the bed. I moved the Scrabble box left out from before dinner and pinned the score sheet to my bulletin board. As he watched he said he had a good time, that he was glad he came.

"Me too," I said. It finally felt true. I was really gay now. It wasn't like before. I wondered when we would be boyfriends. Maybe we'd pick the same school. Our parents would get along. We both went to church. We could come out together. We wouldn't have to travel far for holidays. It made sense. I was seventeen. We talked about the stars on the ceiling that still glowed dimly. My room was small, something he noticed when he arrived. I thought about the sailboat comforter on my bed, a captain's bed, to save room. The shelves were lined with books from my childhood, board games and animals stuffed underneath.

"Are you really gonna go to sleep?" he asked.

The emotions of the day had exhausted me. I couldn't muster a response.

"Well, I'll just come down there," he said, laughing.

Used to his pace now, this time there was no rattle of teeth. I felt his weight on top of me. I reached up and turned the lock, just in case. Between breaths I took in his smell of chlorine, still there from his weeks of swim practice. I held the back of his head, gripping his hair and skull. He moved his hands lower, and I moved them back up. He asked if I was nervous to "do stuff" with a guy for the first time. I had prepared my response to this question in advance. "I just don't want to do any of that tonight," I told him.

"Well, it doesn't *feel* that way," he said. For years I'd been ashamed of this way my body responded. I thought about Sunday school. A teacher telling us about his cousin who was recently diagnosed with AIDS. How God gave it to him, how he deserved it. About the signs those men held that said God hated men like me.

Am I gonna die from this?

Marc kissed me again before he moved back up to the bed. I stayed on the floor, then reached back up and unlocked the door.

DISGREGATE

"It's beautiful in my head, why can't I just throw that onto the page?" I ask aloud. I'm trying to swirl my ideas into something pretty & sensical.

The fridge is black so I add to it as much color as possible. I spell out new words with magnets & wait to see if my partner notices; to see if I can conjure new feelings out of stale ones. Absentmindedly, they speak for me.

BREATHE

SIGH

I thought of something that happened three years ago & audibly groaned.

I make a similar noise in therapy & the therapist calls it the word we're all sick of: "trauma," how I'm stopping myself from thinking about all those nights, all those years.

How it's physiological, exerted through my lungs & out of my throat. How to imagine new feelings out of the old.

◆

Questions that crossed my mind today: *How much does a geography shape a gender? How much does time influence a self?*

When I was in fourth grade, I made it to the Southwest Missouri regional spelling bee. I won my school district's competitions with ease & spent the near entirety of spring studying a long list of words I'd never seen before.

It wasn't as magical as it was on TV—all memorization, a word bank, & some linguistic cues I was too young to fully fathom.

Over break, for a few glorious days, my friends & I zoomed across grass & concrete, exhausting the neighborhood backyards. As if we'd last forever.

+

Who would I be if I could undo the thing I hate most about myself?

One evening, lubricated with alcohol, I grow more emotionally intimate with a friend, then cower away the next day. They are grateful for our conversation full of tears & what felt like revelation, but I avoid their invitation to something outdoors.

I can't stir up a good reason, but sometimes I worry I'm afraid of even small changes—even in positive directions.

I think about calling my friend J who I've not spoken with in a while, but I can't bring myself to press the call button. Like I imagine he thought of me in college, I don't want him to think I'm flighty & sporadic.

I imagine him seeing my name on his phone, muttering "Now what is he calling about?" I imagine an eye roll, too. What if I call & it changes things? Sometimes I dream that we are husbands.

SPILL

Still, there's one boy I fear may never stop leading my nightmares. The worst part is he's always nice in them. You could think he's a good guy.

·

One by one, the other students misspelled their words. It wasn't that I was smarter than them, but that I'd given up more ounces of me to care. My grandmother was in the audience. It was when she could still remember who I was.

Two things were certain that day: she loved me even though we looked nothing alike; I'd buy a PlayStation with the winnings if I won. Life was as simple as that.

On the fridge, I try to be both humorous & aspirational:

ZERO GAYS TODAY

When I'm sick of the other gay colleague.

NO WAR

When I'm sick of the news.

✦

Recently my mother asked me *are you embarrassed of where you come from?* & I didn't know how one was supposed to accurately measure such a feeling.

My father tells takeout orders into the receiver like he's telling a secret. I tell my own quiet & hurried as if I learned from him. Some days, I am a hushed skeleton held together by splintered selves. Most days, I am more than this, but too often I forget.

Other things I dislike about myself: I am never fully unpacked; I don't care for keeping my desk tidy; I work a side job where I pretend to be another person. In it, I give pasted responses & it's funny how often people don't seem to care. "Yes, I'm real, I just use copy and paste to reply more quickly." It's a half truth, which for a paycheck is enough. We're helping people, so there is no harm. But I do get stopped in my tracks when someone catches on & asks—*"Are you a real person?"*

NOT REAL

✦

"Would you fight for what you want?" a woman sings & asks me

through my speakers. "Would you
let it go?"

Or, how the therapist puts it, "what
if you tried being kind to yourself?"

If you want to know how much
currency whiteness is worth, one
must only log onto Twitter. Or
apply for a job.

Or, have you ever seen a political
cartoon so racist you stay in bed
all morning? When trying to
articulate the worst feeling ever—
having witnessed this thing I
knew existed, that nevertheless felt
unimaginable— I cry. *People laugh
at this. Out in the open!* Someone
takes the time to draw these things.

PROTECT US

Today's lesson: People want to
see Black folks miserable & they
don't even realize it. They want you
miserable & when you finally are,
they're still unsatisfied.

I didn't win that day. We ran out of words on the first list so they manifested a new one. I rolled the verb *disgregate* around in my mouth for months after losing to it. In adulthood, it's no longer part of my vocabulary because most people will assume I mean something else. Even the computer suggests an alternative.

D IS G R E G A TE D

It finds its way onto the fridge too.

In the nursing home, when we visited her, my grandmother didn't know what to do with me. She seemed to only be able to place me if my dad was next to my mother— her daughter—& me next to them. This sounds sad, but some days I just think it means that proximity can be quite comforting.

AWE FULL NOT AWFUL

✦

My partner notices my fridge
words are growing moodier: letters
turned poetic lines & black space,
time all overlapping & scrambled.

LOVE IS KIND
        A   OF ★ILLING

I switch the star out for different
letters on different days.

BOOKSHELF
ELEVEN NINE SIXTEEN

I retreat to a room because I can't bear other people; I know what's coming. I lay curled in a bed that's not mine, turn on the fan function of the AC to hear myself think, or not. Try not to wonder if they discuss me, me tired with black and queer in the room. The two compound on each other and make me heavy. I close my eyes.

A few hours earlier, a room discussed a piece I'd written, about the time a group of men called me nigger, repeatedly. The professor asked me if this was *atypical* where I was from. I didn't know how to answer. I wondered if it matters whether it's the first time or the last time a life is threatened. Nothing feels atypical anymore. I can't seem to remember how the day started.

My boyfriend comes to check on me in his bed. Says, I love you, unprompted for the first time. I didn't expect it to sound with an air of fearful protection. In the other room, the map on television is turning all red. We kiss, me under him under the covers. *I love you too.* He leaves. I see a space between the wall and the bookshelf I never noticed before.

I lose sense of time, though when he returns he says, Don't die okay. This means it's over, the map has bled enough. I've never seen tears in his eyes before now, though I've wanted to. Here our difference is named, then skirted around, which, perhaps, is the same thing. The attempt to articulate difference is never finished. I'm tired of writing things others have questions about.

There is a distance between our griefs. A diameter in units I can't quite name. First noticed after Orlando, our mutual pain something we'd have to orbit around, though on different tracks. In the summer I didn't know how to tell him, though I think he knew: I couldn't cry in front of him, because of my pride. I had to wait until I was around people who looked like me.

I'm not sure why tonight someone wanted a party. I wonder if when the world ends, I'd rather be alone.

+

I wake in the morning after something like sleep. Yes, it was real, and I'm alive, though I'm afraid to be. The hole in my stomach reminds me—Orlando, Michael Brown, Trayvon Martin. How strange I can almost forget the feeling of things I've mourned from my bed. They have a way of returning some mornings. I put on my jeans, drive home in the rain.

On the crowded bus three students talk in a triangle around me. Discussing the banks and the economy, laughing at how ridiculous it all is. I can't tell if they voted for him or not, which is enough to tell me that they cannot be trusted. The rest of the bus is quiet, and they are talking so loud. Their emotions are a white heat around them. I loosen when they step off by the private university.

I'm supposed to teach a room full of students in an hour. I don't have the heart to do it, so I send them an email saying *class will be optional*. Without saying it, I say I'm the only black one in the room, can't be the one, today. I don't tell the department, don't want them to ask questions I'm not equipped to answer.

I arrive, knowing some stragglers will not have opened the email. I let the room know, really, they can leave now, I don't want to be *here*. They think I just mean the room. A few kids stay the whole time. They talk about registering for the upcoming semester.

I don't want to see people, but I drop a cable off in my office. Avoid the group of sad white people talking about what they did today in class. Get caught in a question, *what did you say to your students?* I back toward the exit. *I need to go home and sleep.*

I drop my dress clothes on my floor and roll onto bed. Everything hurts a little more. The boyfriend calls to make sure I'm still alive. Yes, I say, though, I'm ambivalent.

QUEST

In grade school, my family took our annual summer vacation to Kansas City, Missouri, driving two hours north to a hotel-casino. In the mornings, we'd leave our room and my parents would head down to gamble, but not before checking me into the hotel's childcare called Kids Quest—a massive, odyssey of an indoor playground with a gigantic play-place, a videogame area, a snack section, and a movie room.

Kids Quest seemed magical and dreamlike. Too, it was a bit of a distraction from my adolescent anxieties. The pastor at church often spoke of the "sinful" nature of gambling, so this was a way to divert myself, to avoid the fear that my parents were doing something I was told was bad. I didn't understand why, if a pastor said not to, my parents didn't feel bad about doing it. I wasn't mad at them, mostly just scared for our collective eternal salvation; I didn't think our household could afford anything else tipping the scales. By age 11, I knew that I was probably gay and that there were parts of myself I wanted to keep hidden. I'd hoped that maybe I'd been dreaming them all up.

I had so much fun at Kids Quest. There I could be the explorer and excavator of my own life each day for a set number of hours. I rarely made friends with stranger kids, knowing that there could always be a risk— their actions unpredictable—instead opting to explore on my own. Each summer I returned, I'd go into the play-place and hit my usual spots: I'd climb up the roller slides and traverse neon colored plastic and vinyl, cascading in its hot pinks, teal blues and deep purples. One year, I discovered a turret I'd never found before, in a spot I'd previously thought too difficult to get to. I poked my head in at the base and peered up. What I saw startled me—at the very tip of the tower, I thought I saw the face of a little girl bathed in dim, lavender light. I asked, *Hello?* She didn't budge. Confused and afraid, I left.

I imagined a child getting trapped up there. No one to find her when all the lights turned off and the venue closed. Her body frozen in perpetuity. No one to notice she was gone. I reasoned that I must have imagined it, but the turret haunted me and followed me back home. I told my parents what I thought I might have seen. They assured me that, if a kid had gone missing, the workers would have searched for them. That parents come to check out their kids. That even if the parents abandoned their child, someone would have noticed when no one came to pick her up. They'd have searched every corner and turret in the place.

This made me feel better but didn't change that I thought I'd seen someone. I tried praying about it. *Dear God, if that was a girl up there in that turret, I hope that she's okay now, or if she's dead, that it didn't hurt. That she didn't feel lonely, or if she's a ghost, that she finds peace. That you let her be with you now even if she was bad. Even though it was at a casino. Even if she sinned and didn't ask for forgiveness enough times. I hope that her family isn't sad anymore & that nothing so awful ever happens again. Amen.* I was an anxious child, and anxious in my prayers.

A year later, the last year before I'd age out of Kids Quest, I decided I must see once and for all if what I'd seen was real. Had a girl just been playing up there? Was she pulling a trick on me? Was she taking a nap? I went up the roller slide. Jumped across foam and mesh. Traversed vinyl and plastic to find that turret again. When I got there, I poked

my head in and looked up. Scared,
I saw the same shadows, the same
lavender, dull light. My stomach
lurched, thinking that such horror
could actually exist. But a year
older, I realized—it was a mirror.
It was only me.

HERE
DISPATCHES FROM A TINY HOUSE

Once again, I am at the whims of the weather. This must become a daily practice. In fear of things getting hotter, I've made myself too cold. Cold in a literal and figurative sense. I'll spare you any false pretense: every move I make anticipates a certain climatic future.

The sun rose this morning but was overcast by clouds. In a set of hours, it will set. This is scientific. Apply that feeling to whichever circumstances of your life, even where you'd least expect. A pessimism. Or simply a routine occurrence. Today's forecast: a nice cool rain; my legs left scrambling chilly beneath a blanket.

✦

The weather, as it does, has affected my dreams. In this one: I forgot my rain jacket, and I've been left sloshing in rain puddles running late for a date. ♠ is in my dreams again. This is typical, but last night I dreamt about ♠ and his older brother. In this one I was choosing between the two of them. One, ♠, whom I'm comfortable with but caused me so much anguish. The other, different in just about every way, but still the brother of ♠.

A dream isn't real life, only an assemblage of memory of me trapped at age ♠-teen. It is climate following me, even states away. A storm brewing out of space and time. A gray squirrel hops in view of the window. Sometimes, crickets chirp even in the daytime.

+

Comfort. I uttered *comfortable* to you earlier, but that might have raised a red flag. See, you spend so much time with someone and they become second nature. Spending years in the wake of someone. So normal and so formative, that my subconscious returns to it more often than anything.

My conception of love's tectonics and platonics have been spliced. Sometimes I still say their name when I mean someone else.

+

Second. Nature. As if we could exhaust this one in exchange for a do-over. Today, the rain dries quicker than expected. I hear a guttural mewl from the trees and when I go to inspect it, I don't find any creature there at all.

In a book I read last night, Dustin Pearson writes, "I didn't think about you for years. I thought about what we did every day."[i] In his book he writes of chickens clucking and laying eggs, chickens as abusers, victims as yolks and I hear one squawking near the premises of the house nearby. Have I mentioned to you yet that there are other people in this place? We don't know what's got the chicken so worked up this morning. I finish the book after. There must be something in the air today.

+

In a film[ii], in present day, a musician drops a mic into a fishing hole in search of sounds with meaning. Together, we, the subject, the filmmakers, the spectator, listen to the sound of ice from decades past as it melts. It is time travel. The musician's creative practice has been disrupted not just by climate anxiety, but the self-destructive nature of humans, the creation of nuclear bombs. He is trying to listen to the natural world around him.

After all this, he is somehow able to make music that's still beautiful in its own right, on instruments made by wood and metal forged by men.

+

The next evening, in a new film[iii], a woman who might be from another planet collapses the lines between what is alien and what is machine. She finds herself to be both things, and a woman. She's not meant to be where she's arrived. She discusses with her new colleague, a journalist, the political warzone they've both found themselves in. How we all—but in this case, Palestinians—are "victims of a map," or man.

Impressed by her resolve and growth across time, her colleague asks how she remains so steady knowing all the knowledge she knows. Her thought is simple and resolute: "It will all end." In the end, she leaves her original mission behind in order to fight for others. She encourages the viewer to do one thing: travel.

A change of scenery can reilluminate one's vision of the world and its order.

✦

I know this is sounding grim, but how might I convince you that this confrontation is helping? That I realize that I am man and this earth is full of altering nature?

If I, one man can do this, maybe you and others can do it to. Maybe it will burst men into action. Maybe we can savor a little more time.

In a ubiquitously popular song in America right now, a singer repeats, "Yeah, I bite my tongue, it's a bad habit."[iv] He imagines a world where he's not afraid to say the thing on his mind the most. Maybe a place can be a new feeling at which to arrive.

✦

Here, it takes only minutes of being away from routine, to see that nature, on the surface, is alive and well. I see what I think is a burst of light, but it's just a busied chipmunk, its warm colors alive and combustible. I watch a handsome blue jay hang out with other birds. On a walk, a lone monarch butterfly flits past me, and then later, another.

Later when we catch the sunset, I notice the leaves of the large tree next to the house are not brown, but a smoldering red. What a rich world there is to witness.

✦

A woman and I explore my body's resistance. How emotion is a *motion*. How it's all connected. We notice there's some resistance in my hips, my pelvis. I think, *of course, this is not surprising,* but I hadn't considered how I carry a trauma with me physically. My past resistance is so rooted in my body it effects my gait.

"You've carried on / acting for so long anyway,"[v] Pearson wrote. So we do exercises where we move my hips and pelvis in three dimensions. She shakes me in motions I've never shook in before. Maybe, just maybe, I can shake this all off, then out.

+

The past few days, I don't dream much of anything. Each day brings to me a new animal I didn't know existed in this environment.

One day it's chipmunks, then turkeys, then crows.

When I'm writing at night, my solar powered light attracts a small winged being. I dislike bugs but don't have the heart to kill this one. Just here, searching for some warmth. What if we took on a practice of keeping everyone alive?

+

I am on the sun's time now. It wakes me when I wouldn't normally want to wake me, and its disappearance lulls me to sleep. I could sit in the sun for hours here, reading. In fact, I do. Fifty pages in and I notice a spider has been on my arm, has begun to spin a tiny web.

I am static, here. I am one with nature. Three birds circle above, sputtering to one another. I know they're not vultures, but I move a little to show them I'm not dead. I am alive.

✦

I've turned red from the light; got caught up in a game of playing with my limits. In an environment so different, I am learner and educator, testing for those of my kind that will come after me. I worry the color will stick, show everyone my recklessness rouged on my face, but in a few hours, it's gone—I a chameleon in this clearing.

✦

Recently, I joked with a poet friend about how Frank Ocean has our generation of Black poets "in a chokehold"—his lyrics always topping our pages, or sprinkled, italicized, in our verse. But it's true he's a bit of a poet. He has an eye for beauty: I listen to him sing as I write[vi], *"Hope our children walk by spring, when flowers bloom / Hope they'll get to see my color, know that I've enjoyed sunshine / Pray they'll get to see me, (me) wither"*

He has an eye for imagining futures. And like the poet, he has a knack for disappearing off the grid.

◆

Today I did something I havern't done in years: watched carefully as a storm approached. I sat in a chair outside in the wind and felt each change in the atmosphere. First, the sun was shining, then gray clouds floated in. It encroached slowly in the beginning. Then suddenly, a bolt of lightning, a steady rain for minutes, then hail. Here nature collapsed in on itself, engulfing everything.

Later, through grids in a screen, I watched three deer graze in the drizzle, at peace.

◆

Grids. Little boxes. Check marks and to-do's. Tick marks marking the hour. It's a shame once you get used to time—what a minute feels like, what it feels like to feel it go. The little blocks begin to take up a physical space.

Today I write about homesickness. I try to explain that this is existential: like life is changing and I can't stop time. I'm not homesick here, but homesick for an adolescent comfort I'm not sure ever existed. I don't want to leave here and go back to Pittsburgh. I'd rather just go straight back to home.

◆

◆, the person I'm sharing this space with for these weeks, also writes about *tormentas*, I discover. But for her, the clouds and the sea might be images of restoration. I can't imagine such a difference in framing, but I begin to trust her. Her name when translated means both sky and sea; I can't believe I didn't notice it before. It was staring me in the face the whole time.

◆

Some neighbors brought us vases of flowers from a garden. They're beautiful, and I imagine a garden with rows and rows of all type of color. Crimson, maroon, a vivid magenta. That there's such color in natural flora, not just in a flower shop, is shocking to me. Some anthers and pollen fall onto my desk and I'm taken with such color. More gold than the sun can ever be.

＋

Jacqui Germain writes[vii] "how fascinating the shape / a city collapses into after it is drained," then later "some body-cities / are only seen when they are screaming."

There were years where I was afraid of the wind: it can be monstrous in its full effect. It can dismantle a home, and can steal someone, so young, that you love. *The clouds are mean*, I thought. In their randomness it comforted people to justify it as not random. How cruel a logic.

But here, in this little house, my fears have dissipated. Not completely gone, but the panic has lessened. If it's my way to go, then so be it. I've already imagined the worst. In my dreams here, I look the storm in the eye. Here, right now, in the breeze, I can almost feel weightless.

＋

A friend whom I've recently reconnected with, ♣, calls out of the blue. He'd done the same about five months ago—until then I hadn't heard his voice in a decade. He was carrying so many things. We came from the same dirt. I tell him things I never told him ten years ago, that I've learned about myself across these days, being outside. It's so easy. It's so natural. When we get off the phone, I'm so happy about it that I cry.

✦

I've made friends with one of the cats. He is black and stays inside but watches through the window, wants to slip past when you open it. One day, when he gets out for the first time, he just steps out only a little, stops where the stone meets the grass in the fresh air.

We have formed a kinship. I can't seem to deny the attention he asks of me. I bring him a blade of green grass to chew on from outside, but he knows it's not the same as when it's growing from the ground.

✦

◆ asks for me to share my favorite show with her. It's a big question but the answer reveals itself. But then, through it, suddenly, I worry I've laid bare some of the most vulnerable parts of me. *This is what entertains me. This is the type of tension that leaves me in awe.*

The subtitles aren't capturing some of the moodiness, I feel. It seems less assured of its own themes in this different language. I worry it will not land with her. I worry what once seemed so deep seems a bit trivial. Still, each night we watch a little more of it. When it's over, we have so much to talk about.

◆

I worry that I've bored you. That the logic of these observations is escaping each of us. But I'm trying to be a stronger person, and for me that's writing things down. For so long, I kept a secret that keeps me up at night. I thought I was comfortable with taking it to my grave, but maybe my body is tired of holding it in. I shrunk into myself. But I've been here thirty years and I want to feel as full and bursting as the roaring skies. I think there's lightning in here, and I'm so close to letting it out.

◆

My best friend from childhood, ♥, calls about her upcoming wedding. I love her so much, yet I feel like it never comes across over the phone. It's been so long since I've seen her. I just need to be in the same room with her, rid myself of the ice and thaw into our love.

Back in Pittsburgh, whenever I'm walking somewhere I think "who can I call that will pick up?" and then don't make a call. Out of my own fear, I spend many walks to the apartment not talking to anyone. Moving forward, I resolve to recenter ♥.

♦

♣ calls again and I'm so shocked I can't seem to formulate a sentence. I worry he thinks I was scared when I saw his name on my phone. I worry that I was. I do the math and it's just been four days. I realize that this is something that might be permanent. A best friend I thought I'd lost forever, back in my life, for good. Did I tell you I'll be seeing him soon? I don't know what he looks like anymore. I don't know if he knows what I look like now. I consider sending him a photo. I don't look like I did when I was twenty.

We only talk for four minutes, but at the end of the call, so quickly, he tells me *I love you.* I didn't expect him to say it, so he hung up before I could respond. But it's true, I do love him back.

♦

That first evening here, ♦ and I watched a movie[viii] that enraptured us. In it, the boy's first queer love didn't love him after all. Or wasn't brave enough to love him. Though who would be in such geography.

I take for granted what small freedoms I'm afforded. But haven't trauma and drawn lines always left people like you and me displaced? Despite these limitations, this boy was so free. He pulsed yellow and red and orange when he danced. He was shimmering. He was man. *He* was the sun, not the men around him. His orbit could pull the tides if they'd let it. His pull could disrupt the skies.

---

[i] From the poem "Letter 13" by Dustin Pearson in *Millennial Roost*

[ii] Ryuichi Sakamoto: *Coda* (2017) directed by Stephen Nomura Schible

[iii] *Friendship's Death* (1987) directed by Peter Wollen

[iv] "Bad Habit" performed by Steve Lacy

[v] From the poem "Choosing Abuse" by Dustin Pearson in *Millennial Roost*

[vi] "Wither" performed by Frank Ocean

[vii] From the poem "On The Chemical Properties & Uses of Dried Blood" by Jacqui Germain in *Bittering the Wound*

[viii] *And Then We Danced* (2020) directed by Levan Akin

NOTES

Each piece in this chapbook was imagined and created with a particular formal or creative constraint.

The epigraph comes from Aisha Sabatini Sloan's *Borealis*.

Works referenced in "Apartmentalization" include the television series *Dare Me, Search Party,* and *The Terror,* and the film *Annihilation* (2018).

Names in "On A Bridge" were changed for privacy. The song referenced in the piece is Say Anything's "I Want to Know Your Plans."

In "Disgregate," the song playing through the speakers is Tinashe's "So Much Better."

ACKNOWLEDGMENTS

Thank you to every person who has shared space with me across the years as these pieces were written.

A special thanks to Outpost and all of its supporters. Thank you to Ricardo Wilson (and Meredith) for giving me the residency space not just to write "Here," but for a space for respite and creation. This chapbook wouldn't exist without that inspiration. I'm forever grateful to have been a fellow, ever chasing that serenity. Mariceu Erthal—thank you for your company, your brilliance.

Thank you to Ander Monson. What an honor—a dream—for this work to find a home at New Michigan Press.

Thank you to Mom and Dad. Thank you to Grandma Jeanie. Thank you, Auburn and Toy. Thank you to all my friends who appear in this work.

Thank you to S. Brook Corfman for your steadfast support.

Thanks to Dāshaun Washington, Jamila Osman, Bernardo Wade, Laura Pegram, Erin Khar, and Maggie Jones, for your support of various works herein. Special thanks to Meredith Talusan who helped in me making sense of pieces in this project and their revision.

Thank you to literary journals where previous versions of these works appear: *Brink, Kweli Journal, Indiana Review, Wildness,* and *The Common Online.*

And thank you to you, dear reader, for spending the time with this work.

STEFFAN TRIPLETT is a Black, queer writer born and raised in southwest Missouri. He is the author of *Bad Forecast* (Essay Press, 2024) and has received fellowships and support from Outpost, Lambda Literary, Callaloo, and Cave Canem. Triplett is the Managing Director of the Center for African American Poetry and Poetics and a Teaching Assistant Professor at the University of Pittsburgh. More of his essays have appeared in *Vulture, Longreads, The Iowa Review,* and *It Came From the Closet: Queer Reflections on Horror* (Feminist Press, 2022).

❁

COLOPHON

Text is set in a digital version of Jenson, designed by Robert Slimbach in 1996, and based on the work of punchcutter, printer, and publisher Nicolas Jenson. The titles here are in Futura, the best font for titles.

❀

NEW MICHIGAN PRESS, based in Tucson, Arizona, prints
poetry and prose chapbooks, especially work that transcends
traditional genre. Together with DIAGRAM, NMP sponsors a
yearly chapbook competition.

DIAGRAM, a journal of text, art, and schematic, is
published bimonthly at THEDIAGRAM.COM. Periodic print
anthologies are available from the New Michigan Press at
NEWMICHIGANPRESS.COM.